THINKABOUT

Floating and Sinking

THINKABOUT

Floating and Sinking

Text: Henry Pluckrose
Photography: Chris Fairclough

Franklin Watts
London/New York/Sydney/Toronto

©1986 Franklin Watts

First published in Great Britain by

Franklin Watts
12a Golden Square
London W1

First published in the USA by

Franklin Watts Inc
387 Park Avenue South
New York 10016

ISBN: UK edition 0 86313 431 9

ISBN: US edition 0–531–10294–7
Library of Congress
Catalog Card No: 87–50229

Editor: Ruth Thomson
Design: Edward Kinsey
Additional Photographs: Zefa

Typesetting: Keyspools Ltd
Printed in Italy
by Lito Terrazzi, Firenze

About this book

This book is designed for use in the home, playgroup, kindergarten and infant school.

Parents can share the book with young children. Its aim is to bring into focus some of the elements of life and living which are all too often taken for granted. To develop fully, all young children need to have their understanding of the world deepened and the language they use to express their ideas extended. This book takes the everyday things of the child's world and explores them, harnessing curiosity and wonder in a purposeful way.

For those working with young children each book is designed to be used both as a picture book, which explores ideas and concepts, and as a starting point to talk and exploration. The pictures have been selected because they are of interest in themselves and also because they include elements which will promote enquiry. Talk can lead to displays of items and pictures collected by children and teacher. Pictures and collages can be made by the children themselves.

Everything in our environment is of interest to the growing child. The purpose of this book is to extend and develop that interest.

Henry Pluckrose.

Water ...
so much water
that it seems to touch the sky.

More water . . .
flowing over the stones
of a tiny river.

Water in a lake,
smooth and motionless.

Water in your bath,
warm and comforting.

Water in the pools
and puddles which come
after heavy rain.

We can do things on land
that we cannot do in water.
We cannot walk on water,
but we can walk through it.

We can do things in water
that we cannot do on land.
We cannot float on land!

These boats are floating on the lake, but boats full of water . . .

sink!

These toys float.
Which toys do you play with in the bath?
Are they toys which always float,
or do they sometimes sink?

Not everything will float.
Will these enormous rocks float
if they fall into the sea?

This bridge is made
of metal girders.
Would they float
if they fell into the river?

These are logs.
Do they float?

This glass bottle has a screw top.
It is filled with air.
Will it sink?

This glass bottle has no top.
If it fills with water,
will it still float?

This can is made of metal.
It contains nothing but air.

What happens if the can fills
with water?
It sinks!
Why do things float?

Air helps things to float . . .
like this rubber balloon,

this buoy

and this toy ship.

All these things are hollow.
If things are hollow,
they are filled with air.

Some things float
because they are lighter
than water, like these leaves.
As the water soaks into them,
they become waterlogged and sink.

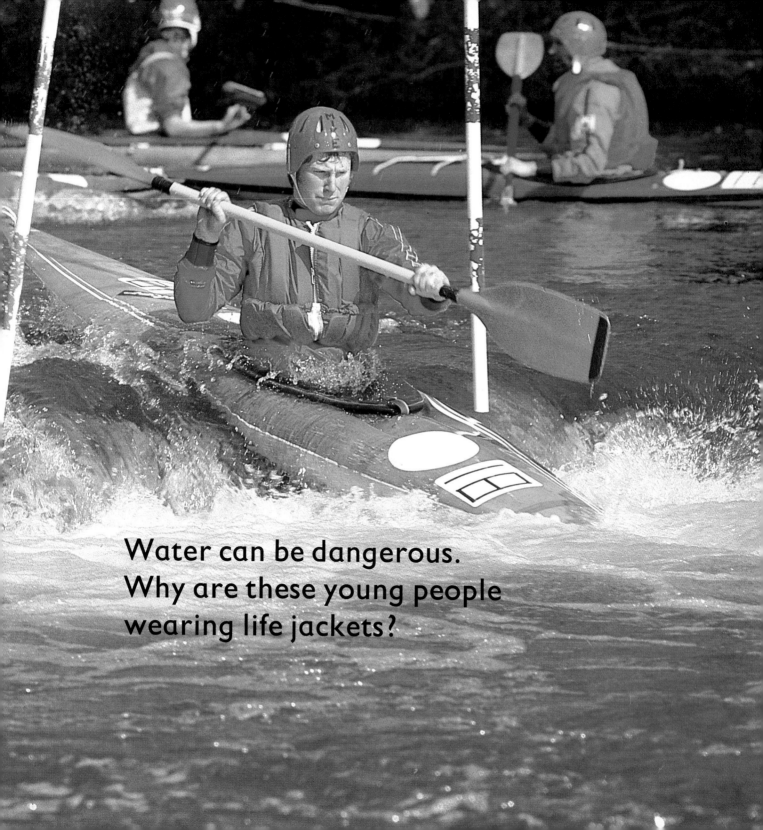

Water can be dangerous.
Why are these young people
wearing life jackets?

Sailors wear
life jackets too!

Which of these things
do you think will sink?

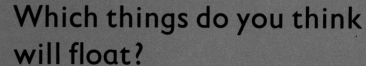

Which things do you think
will float?

Fill a bowl with water.
Drop some things into it.

Why do some things float
and some things sink?